10 STRATEGIES TO CREATE HIGH PERFORMING SALES CULTURE

SALES CULTURE FUELS SALES SUCCESS

ANTHONY CHAINE

HIGH PERFORMANCE SALES MANAGEMENT

∽

In my long experience as a salesperson and leader, I found that what I always needed most were ideas to build high-performance sales teams. Sales management is a tough job. You've got to lead, manage and coach your sales team. You've got to meet or exceed your projected team quota. You're responsible to your customers, peers and business partners. This book is designed to help you address those challenges.

MY ENTIRE BUSINESS career has been in sales and sales management. I've worked with small, mid-sized, national and global businesses. Through my career, I've picked up tens of thousands of experiences. The lessons I've learned have been instrumental in creating high performance, result oriented, winning sales team that thrives under strong sales culture.

My primary goal in writing *10 strategies To Create High*

Performing Sales Culture is to offer an actionable quick guide that sales managers can adapt to increase team productivity.

Stock photo ID:478904385 Credit: Kieferpix

Reality Check

It's the end of the month, and as a sales manager, you are behind on your work quotas, you are worried, stressed out, and the pressure on you is tremendous. Your boss and senior management are waiting for you to turn in your last projections, but you feel horrible, ashamed of your team performance, and you feel you are dragging everyone down. Although you tried your best, you end up coming short because some of your sales reps' outputs were disastrous.

The reports that require your attention are piling up and must be addressed asap. Making matters worse, other departments are waiting for you to turn them in, but you don't have the time even though you spent the last three weekends working to catch up.

Your two new hires are struggling with their work load,

they need your assistance to overcome some pending issues, they also need some orientation and feedback on other urgent topics. But you don't have enough time with all the work you have to do. You wish you could split yourself in multiple parts to help everyone, but that's impossible.

Adding to your problem, you have several open positions that need to be filled, but you just cannot find the right candidates. You have struggling sales reps that require field time coaching, but you keep being dragged in different directions to resolve urgent customers and partners issues!

Your customers are demanding; your partners are unforgiving. Getting new business is incredibly hard. The competition is fierce. Your customer are extremely savvy and educated, and often seem to know more than your salespeople.

Your sales reps are overwhelmed; there are too many customers' issues to resolve, too many reports to generate, and too little time to sell. You feel emotionally down and try to portray an image of control, but in reality, this is highly strenuous environment that imprisons you with its intense demand and constant high pressure. You often wonder if you lack the aptitude, capability, and stamina for the job. You also wonder if your sales force has what it takes to succeed.

Your ability to adapt, analyze on-the-go, and make smart decisions can make the difference between success and failure.

Market demands are high, sales reps needs to be faster, smarter, and more agile than ever before. This means your sales reps needs to have the ability to:

- Self-educate continuously on the product knowledge.

- Absorb a massive quantity of information, reflect on it, simplify it, and deliver it in digestible portions to your customers.
- Upgrade current skills and add new capabilities based on markets trends and clients' demands.
- Become experts at resolving quickly customers issues while reducing tension.
- Get creative to predict escalations and problems and proactively engineer a path to resolution.

Unless you are selling a product or service that is perfect in every sense, and your innovation far exceed consumer demand, your trained sales force is your primary competitive advantage and your greatest asset.

Most companies rely on their salespeople to create revenue in quantity large enough to keep them profitable to grow and expand. Customers rely on salespeople to provide education and insight on a broad range of commerce solutions that allow them to develop a competitive edge.

The most successful salespeople are those who continually generate new ideas, insights, and market data that impact existing and future customers. To acquire new business, sales reps have to provide unique alternatives beyond the obvious to entice the customer into considering and accepting the offer.

It begs the question: Are all members of the team equipped to win the sales battle?

To ensure a seamless transition from the current status-quo to higher standards, the sales manager may have to change the sales culture. Underperformance needs to be addressed, sales reps who are not willing to do their part to achieve their objective need to be faced head-on. Laggers may need some pushing and pulling to get them to achieve better results. The key is to challenge everyone to get out of the status-quo. The top sales reps may need to be encouraged and shown different alternatives that may lead to greater performance.

By following the strategies outlined below, you can turn your current sales team from the slow-moving and reactive state to a higher state of proactive learning and greater performance

1. YOUR CHALLENGES ARE OPPORTUNITIES TO SUCCESS - YOUR JOB IS TO EXPLOIT THEM

Welcome your challenges and issues. These are learning opportunities that you can turn into winning propositions.

Sales is regarded as one of the hardest jobs on the planet. Hard because it undergoes a constant evolution that requires continuous education, fast adaptability, complex issue resolution, and flexible psychological approaches that retain and improve the relations with your customers.

The sales manager and his salespeople work under constant pressure to deliver on the required company quota. The cycle is simple; every new month you go from a hero to zero. Not continually achieving your quota means the loss of bonus, status, and potentially the job for both your sales reps and possibly you — the sales manager.

You certainly feel anxious when new promising and disruptive products come to the market, you know your team will need to adapt fast or you will lose market share. You get worried when new competitors hit the market with new product/services that your company cannot match quickly enough, you feel powerless and at a disadvantage.

You lose sleep when you have a couple of consecutively bad quarters; underperformance is an existential threat for sales management.

You turn to your sales reps for what you hope is good news, to your surprise you are faced with a barrage of complaints and excuses, ranging from: "I cannot meet the quota this month because my customer is considering a last minute request for proposal that offers additional values at a lower cost," to "the customer has suddenly become unresponsive, wants more time, or has financial challenges." whether, legitimate reasons or plain excuses, it doesn't matter you know you have a gap that needs immediate resolution. You also realize that your sales reps are operating with a sense of lost hope, and you are stuck.

What should you do when everything seems to take a turn for the worse?

Every problem is a challenge, and every challenge represents an opportunity to be resolved. Fortunes are made that way.

Some of these issues may include:

- Low sales and potentially demanding customers.
- Customers requiring high maintenance needs that the sales rep can't meet.
- Salespeople keep selling the old way although the market demand has shifted.
- New business-acquiring methodology is no longer effective and needs an upgrade.
- Sales reps are sacrificing margin to win new business, generating non-profitable sales.
- The team is comprised mostly of order takers, doing whatever the customer requests.

The majority of sales leaders panic when faced with

multiple issues and the potentiality of missing quota. It's common that sales managers go into an offensive mode to disrupt sales reps complacency. They start giving directives to the their sales reps, while closely micro-managing behaviors and results. Some sales managers start asking and even pleading with their sales reps to work harder, to be more proactive, in term of calls and opportunity management. However, without newly outlined ideas, one should expect the same results. Asking a strained sales force to work harder may sound good, but rarely generates the intended results. Aimless hard work took them to where they are today; what they need is guided coaching to allow them to find a new momentum.

Requesting your sales reps to work harder is simply a misguided strategy that will not generate any appeal or additional action.

Great sales leaders always identify the nature and source of the challenge at hand. Then, they reflect on the challenge as if it were an opportunity. Once the challenge is understood and evaluated, the question becomes: How can we resolve it and benefit from this experience going forward?

This strategy works because it brings people together to brainstorm and solve the challenge by using collective experiences and creativity.

"What can we do together to resolve this current production problem and how can we benefit from it to push ourselves forward?"

For example, your team sales productivity are inadequate because a new competitor has entered the market with a product that is cheaper or perceived better than yours.

The solution?

- Get your team together, and begin drafting a strategy that will retain your existing customers base, while expanding it via customer satisfaction excellence.
- Create a program that involves and reward your existing customers referrals. Get the team to focus on the newly referred prospects by bundling additional added-value solutions that appeal to the new prospects.
- Conduct a regional customer based market survey to find out how to compete against your competitor product advantages.

You should brainstorm with your team members around potential solutions that will address the current challenges. Using a series of logical steps, you should be able to find multiple solutions. The key is to encourage and respect your team and customers market feedback.

This approach will serve you well, regardless of the nature and size of the problem. It provides you with new ways to capitalize on challenges every time. The new ideas will stimulate your thinking power and will enhance team cohesiveness. It inspires everyone to action, and it will impact team performance.

2. FAILURE IS THE WAY TO SALES EXCELLENCE. FAILURE SHOULD BE REPLACED BY "TEACHING" MOMENTS.

To create high performing sales culture and attain sales excellence, you will need to manage your sales team on how to handle both successes and failures well.

Sales excellence is attained through sales leadership that does more than just set goals. It requires a precise balance of good management and targeted coaching. Team performance depends on clear, focused, and efficient sales leadership.

Deals are lost because of multiple reasons. No deals is secure until booked, approved, and activated. No amount of planning or execution on the part of the salesperson can guarantee a sale. The sales rep may be an influencer, but the buying decision is always made by the decision maker. Losing opportunities is part of the sales process. However, understanding the reason on why the deal was lost is important so the same mistake is not repeated.

New hires should not reprimanded for making mistakes; the lesson learned are simply priceless and will serve as guideposts on the path to success. As a sales manager, you should coach your sales reps that mistakes are part of life. The key is to explore, experiment, and avoid repeating the same mistakes. Learn and pass on the knowledge to others that the willingness to fail and overcome adversity, makes you stronger.

Failure-sharing among team members should be encouraged, discussed, and dissected. Solutions should be considered, implemented, and recorded to ensure that the team has a reference book on how to avoid business pitfalls and resolve unique challenges. Deliberate, collective feedback should be an ongoing process to improve team performance.

Junior sales reps often share their mistakes with the rest of the team to get clarity and guidance. Tenured sales reps make occasional juniors mistakes, but often fail to share them with others because of negative perception factors.

The sales manager job is to ensure everyone understands that mistakes will occur, but the wisdom learned from these mistakes must be shared with everyone to avoid costly reoccurrence. Being ego-free and humble can create an environment that promotes the following:

- Review and discuss how sales failures can be tools to be leveraged to lead to sales excellence.
- Explain the relationship between success and failures and the behaviors that leads to improved performances.
- Discuss the sales leader and sales reps' roles on sharing and learning from each other's wins and losses.
- Salespeople and organizations learn from their mistakes.

- Explain the value of failure; reaching out and stretching beyond your comfort zone have potent benefits. Breakthrough innovations stem from major failures.
- Failures should be addressed only as *teaching moments,* necessary for growth and creativity.

Here is the truth: you only have "wins" and "teaching" moments. Instruction and reinforcement should happen as often as possible to ensure it becomes part of the team DNA.

As a sales leader, you will need to do the following:

Prep the unprepared

Ensure that your sales reps are always prepared in terms of careful reflection, planning, and execution. Discuss possible questions and curved approaches, and envision what matters to the customer most to prevent surprises. Brainstorm on individual abilities to benefit the rest of the team, and adopt collective best practices to handle stressful situations as they occur.

Extract lessons from every teaching moment.

Analyze what occurred and ask what could have been done better. Discuss the *how* and capitalize on this occurrence. Turn temporary setbacks into a new possibilities and create an action plan to address future similar lapses.

Learn and move on.

Recognize gaps, opportunities, and create winning action plan. Harness the power of collective team thinking. Create a path to address similar challenges in the future and get on with the next challenge.

"Every crucial experience can be regarded either as a setback or the start of an incredible new adventure; it depends on your perspective!" – Mary Roberts Rinehart, mystery writer

Being a great sales leader is all about distilling value and feedback from setbacks as well as learning great lessons from the experience. Great teams share the good and bad, you have to cultivate the habit of sharing to allow collective, genuine improvement . Winning is the purpose, but you cannot win unless you learn how to improve each player game to enhance the team collective game.

3. CREATE AN ENVIRONMENT THAT SUPPORTS STRETCH TO EXCELLENCE

To reach maximum performance, you will need performers who act like they cannot fail and who constantly stretch beyond their potential zone. You will need engaging, relentless, faithful sales warriors. But how can you create that sales culture without losing everyone in the process?

If you push too hard, you will create a culture of defensive sales reps that will justify failures with all types of excuses and even reasons to save face.

You certainly do not want to push too hard or too fast, as you may damage the team balance and may jeopardize the relationship with your sales reps. It may be prudent to deploy a slower, sustainable and progressive approach to produce stable and long-term results.

Sales reps need a healthy working environment that promotes growth, through nurtured leadership guidance. Talent productivity necessitates continuous coaching, education, and feedback. Sales reps may not have enough confidence to go beyond their comfort zone, but a good sales manager challenges everyone to achieve what was deemed impossible in the past. Every achievement that crosses new boundaries opens the horizon to new possibilities and new conquests.

Stretch goals can be achieved by assisting your reps to recognize their strengths and focus on one or two priorities to reach mastery levels within these areas.

Here is how you can do it:

Define the area of improvements that each particular rep can work upon within a reasonable period and which will have the highest impact on performance, morale and finance.

Stretch zone attainment model and process.

Step 1: Vision is the way

- Define the vision and path forward.
- Build consensus and passion around the vision.
- Your vision should be the signpost that keeps everyone on the pre-set path to success.
- Set the cadence, create momentum and monitor progress closely.

Step 2: Define the path together

- Set collective and individual objectives.
- Establish the plan to get there.
- Identify the required daily action and disciplines.
- Inspect execution, evaluate, reflect, and adjust based on progress.
- Assist by eliminating barriers, coach, inspect, and encourage everyone to stay the course.

Step 3: Lead from the front

- Be the motivational in-chief, and inspire the team consistently.
- Take initiative with your best players to define best practices, then share with the team and monitor execution.
- Provide one-on-one coaching as often as necessary.
- Create and demand willful team collaboration.
- Hire, attract, and retain top talent.
- Celebrate victories, keep team moral up, and create a sales culture that promotes sharing of ideas, insight, experience, and best practices.
- Show gratitude, thank your team members frequently. Look at them always as equals.

Always be on the lookout for talented individuals who can add value to the team. Develop your new talent, look beyond activities and skill gaps. Good sales managers influence belief and behavior to create confident sales performers. Ensure that you have a system that allows new hires to ramp up quickly.

The training system should be methodical, gradual, and easy to grasp. The purpose is to create sales reps that can influence decision makers in a consultative way that will allow them to see the value of the proposed business solution.

4. INCREASE THE EFFECT OF BRAND IMAGE

Brand credibility increase sales.

Whether you manage an outside or inside sales force, your ability to enhance the brand image of your company's products and services can dramatically improve team morale and the ability to achieve specified quota. As a sales leader, you must ensure that your sales reps position the brand they represent correctly during each and every interaction with their clientele. Each communication with a client is an honest opportunity to market the company and an opportunity to listen to the customer feedback, which will be reported back to senior management. Client intel is the most valid information that defines the future of any organization. Customer behaviors, needs and wants drive organizational direction.

Customer perspective focuses on the perceptions based on ease of usage, simplicity, received value, interactions with the sales rep, family and friend experiences, and market vibes.

4. INCREASE THE EFFECT OF BRAND IMAGE

Great sales leaders are attuned to their clients' needs and track their insights carefully to create value innovation and progress. Ignoring customers critical feedback is sure way to demonstrate you are slow and out-of-touch.

The following questions could be just a start:

- Are we meeting our client's satisfaction criteria—through their eyes?
- How do our clients view value our innovation delivery?
- What other values can we deliver to our customers in a cost-effective manner?
- Why is it critical to enhance our brand image with every sales rep interaction?
- How to turn satisfied customers into brand ambassadors?
- How to increase customer retention, loyalty, and new referrals?
- What needs to occur to increase repeat business and client portfolio mix?
- What can be done to increase our market share on new verticals?
- What strategy need to be implemented to generate new partnerships and improve community relationship?
- How to to increase brand awareness?
- What is our market perception?
- Does our brand name open or close doors?

What Else Does Brand Image Affect? **Business Metrics:**

4. INCREASE THE EFFECT OF BRAND IMAGE

- Grow revenue, increase profits and shareholder value.
- Reduce costs, improve financial position and overall leadership attraction and retention.

Team Performance:

- Employees love to work for known corporate brands. It improves morale, cohesiveness, and harmony among team members.
- Increase efficiency, spur the desire to acquire new knowledge and skills to growth within the company.
- Improve employee retention, increase profitability and revenue — Tenured reps produce higher margins . Brand appeal creates demand.
- Shorten the sales cycle and increase sales velocity.

5. EXPERIMENT WITH COLLABORATIVE LEADERSHIP IN THE FIELD

Creating a culture of excellence is all about team collaboration, with a continual focus on getting better at maximizing the performance of each sales rep within the team. The best way to do it is by engaging, coaching, educating, teaching, learning, and inspiring individuals and the team to achieve common goals.

Great sales managers manage hearts, emotions, and behaviors to affect attitude, energy, and people psychology. Alternatively, average sales managers believe that they can influence people and performance by managing primarily data and reports. Analytical reports provide the sales manager with a snapshot on the current team performance. Armed with this data, the sales manager can use available tools and strategies to affect team activity and redirect sales reps focus, which in turn will improve sales productivity metrics.

However, no amount of data analysis, reporting, or performance reviews can impact performance as intended. These activities simply give you a false sense of managing individuals' developments. You cannot coach your sales reps unless you spend time interacting with them in a face-to-face setting or in the field observing their interactions and behaviors.

Data and reports are facts that need to be analyzed and evaluated often to affect needed performance changes. A sales rep who shows low net new business penetration may need to increase his prospecting by potentially identifying and targeting specific verticals within a specific geography. Sales reps who reflect low revenue may need some guidance on how to focus on larger opportunities with higher margins.

The sales manager's responsibility is to get each sales rep to meet and exceed his quota. However, each sales rep will need to know what's expected from him and how to get to his objectives.

Successful sales managers must listen, understand, and connect with their sales reps at a deeper level. This activity will allow the team to deliver better performances, because they feel like they are part of an organization that cares about their well-being and general improvement.

Employee satisfaction is extremely important; people want to work for a sales leader and a sales organization that value their contributions, input, ideas, and potential. Customer satisfaction has a direct correlation with employee satisfaction. Happy employees go above and beyond to serve customers, they often make it easier to do business with, they wow the customer, which triggers customer referrals and great reviews on social media. Satisfied employees work harder, they accomplish much more within the same working hours. They help their peers by sharing best practices and winning strategies. Astute sales managers facilitate interaction among sales reps, breed a sense of genuine camaraderie and enthusiasm and foster a sense of competitive spirit.

6. SALES ARE DOWN! EXAMINE THE MAN IN THE MIRROR

Growth has stalled, revenue has stalled. You are now under the magnifying glass. Everyone is looking at you, and you are stressed. You don't know how to resolve this dilemma. Is it a market shift? A failed marketing strategy? Are your sales reps chasing the wrong opportunities? Maybe they are targeting the wrong verticals with declining potential and appeal?

Alarmed senior management may start asking you, what's happening to your team? Is it a training issue? A behavioral issue? A marketing issue? or is it you? You start to panic think, my sales reps are doing everything they can to drum up business. We have several deals in the funnel at different stages, but we are getting resistance to close these deals. We lost a key customer lately, even though we tried our best to retain him. The competition seems fierce and unstoppable. Our new product launch has been too slow and riddled with technical issues that created major client frustration and require the sales reps to assist instead of focusing on new sales.

Based on your experience, you know that salespeople do

not cope well with insecurities. They do not deal well with sudden shifts in organizational directions, and they certainly do not do well when they are being blamed for others' missteps. Salespeople often feel that other supporting cross-functional departments such as Finance, Credit and Marketing are not supportive. Hence, creating anxiety as salespeople depend on them to facilitate the sales process and contribute to customer service excellence.

Salespeople are wired to adapt to complex environments, however, adaptation takes effort, distract from objectives. Sales managers should understand individual trigger and lead the team through complexity and uncertainty to achieve the required goals.

- What are the company strategic goals?
- How can you help the team accomplish them?
- How can you overcome your competitors' products advantage?
- How can you grow your key account?
- Who can educate the team on how to achieve sales objectives?
- What sales activities should you focus on?
- Are your sales reps equipped for battle?
- Are they trained and ready to execute?
- Do your sales reps know how to eliminate resistance and close deals?
- Are your sales reps committed to win while providing great customer service?

Sales leaders must understand that the quality of their salespeople and level of preparation defines the revenue outcome for the whole organization. All senior management across functions must realize they all depend on their client's revenue to expand and prosper. The only door to growth is to retain existing customers and expand the existing portfolio through new business acquisition.

That means everyone depends on sales to create revenue, and the organization's success depends on the strength of the sales organization. Healthy sales organization create healthy sales cultures.

7. MOVING BEYOND QUOTA ACHIEVEMENTS TO ENSURE MULTI-DIMENSIONAL PERFORMANCES

Congratulations! Your team has achieved quota, and you are all making bonuses! Is that all?

Upon close inspection, client retention is terrible. The sales people attrition is at fifty percent, and you must compress margin to compete. You are barely achieving revenue growth.

You do not feel at ease, and when you dig deep, it feels like you are standing in quicksand. You are not wowing your clients and you are losing your existing large customers to your competitors. To top it, you are losing market share at an alarming pace, the customer service is below par, and the functionality of your products/services is average. You are behind in production efficiency and delivery effectiveness. While you are keeping afloat, you know that the grounds upon which you stand is crumbling. Should you focus on quota attainment or ensure that the field intelligence is shared with senior management to consider? I think you know the answer.

Sales leaders should always focus on the multi-dimensions that facilitates performances. Organizations often get lost in the moment; they need thoughtful sales leaders who regularly provide feedback, insight, and directions to allow the top management to strategize and adjust. The organization's success is in the hands of everyone, regardless of the job or title.

No one should rest on his or her laurels whether the quota is attained or not; predicting market trends and facing current market reality is the job of every sales leader. Hitting goals is a short-term indicator, sustained sales objectives achievement is the goal.

Healthy financial, gain of market share, and customer satisfaction should be the ultimate goal, the latter are the long-term indicators of any healthy business. History has shown that several companies went out of business even though they showed acceptable business results. Studies have shown that these companies never predicted sudden market shift or innovative disruptive technologies that changed demand dynamics.

The way companies had operated in the past is no longer the way the customer, interact, consume information, shop or self-educate. Customer behavior is changing fast, buying behaviors are influenced by many social media factor, company brand, review scoring, attention span is getting shorter, it short it's getting harder to sell unless the company is reaching to its potential prospects via multi-channel with customized content and great context.

Great sales leaders focus tactically on the team activities to ensure continued progress and goal attainment, but they also gather field intelligence and feedback to keep a pulse on all the potential threats that can disrupt their industry.

8. ALWAYS REWARD YOUR SALESPEOPLE ACHIEVED SUCCESS

You are hot, your team is killing it this month, you cannot believe your team production, everyone seems to be riding high. Achievement of this magnitude seems unreal. You constantly cross check the numbers and validate progress. You are pumped because you know your boss is going to be proud, and he may even ask you to share your strategy with other sales leaders so they can share and reinforce the same behavior with their team members. When this reality occurs, it behooves you to reward your sales reps appropriately for their hard work.

There are many ways you can reward them. You can choose between:

- Recognize publicly your top producers for a job well done.
- Allow your top performers to educate the rest of the team.
- Offer a paid day off.
- Offer a paid meal delivery for a week.
- Consider monetary rewards.

- Send a thank you note with gift card.
- Take them out for a congratulatory dinner with your boss.
- Allocate a company-paid weekend vacation.
- Consider top producer for future project or promotions

Many companies organize awards at the end of the year, and they reward whichever sales team or salesperson has been most productive throughout the year. Many send their top five percent to President Club where they have a wonderful time with their partners and look forward to join the next year.

Salespeople love rewards, they work hard to achieve financial rewards, but many work hard for the joy of recognition that stimulates their ego and pumps their pride. These are intrinsic attributes; however, they are just as important as a financial gain. Many salespeople work hard to join the rank of leadership, so there should be a clear path for anyone that exudes the right managerial required attributes.

Incentives are powerful motivation factors. Salespeople will work twice as hard to be recognized for extraordinary achievements. Job title change can be a great motivator as well. For example, promoting someone from an account executive to a senior account executive can make a huge difference in the way they perceive themselves. Adding a financial bonus to that achievement will trigger the desire of other sales reps to achieve the same rights. I have witnessed a huge spike in productivity in a company that simply allocated a special assistance number to its top sales force reducing the wait time to get assistance. The sales reps that have access to this quicker live help were thrilled with the service, so they promoted it internally. Everyone wanted to become part of that top five percent just to access that privilege. Sales spiked because of it. The company almost double its sales force productivity because of it.

Another company sent its top ten winners along with their family into an all paid weekend trip to exotic places. The quarterly winners had scored top place in one specific revenue bucket, allowing people to win by focusing on different bucket that the company wanted to drive. Results were phenomenal, and the energy was contagious, as everyone has a chance to win a family all-paid-expense every quarter.

Similar creative action is an excellent way to bring out optimum productivity from your sales team because they will feel like they are recognized and valued. Smart strategies as the above get you to have teams of sales reps firing on all guns, and you get to have healthy competition in the work environment.

9. ORGANIZE REGULAR TRAINING EXERCISES FOR YOUR TEAM

If you try to read back, you will see I mentioned that the business climate is a dynamic environment. Almost every force in life affects the business industry. New regulation announcements, climate issues, political turmoil or even stocks drop might significantly affect the business industry for a specific period.

There is absolutely no room for inflexibility as times change, and people must change with the times or risk being left behind.

If you don't constantly update your knowledge and are still actively in business, then your success is questionable at best. To stay profitable, you will need to keep your sales team up to speed in terms of new business trends and marketing strategies.

As a sales leader, you will need to organize regular training sessions for the development of your staff. You will also need to encourage them to grow and get better and adapt to shifting trends in the market.

Let's face it, a workshop is usually a dull affair that focuses on productivity. Many salespeople despise training unless it creates value that sets them apart from their counterparts. However, when the training is well organized, stimulating, and engaging, salespeople will look forward to it. General Electric is known to have amazing training, people look forward to them as they experience the added-value derived from them.

Good training improves capability in core areas. It expands knowledge of salespeople, it addresses weaknesses in workplace skills, improves performance, creates consistency, increase salespeople job satisfaction, and it creates internal business connectivity and harmony.

10. TRIM OFF THE DEADWOOD

Whether you like it or not, perennial under-performers will need to go. They are toxic to be around top performers. Get real and terminate them. They are slowing down everyone else, and they are eroding the team moral. Your legacy has to do with how you tolerate and manage these perennial under-performers. If you have done everything humanly possible to turn them around and they simply didn't have the necessary will to swim of their own, make the right tough decision and let them go.

As the saying goes "A chain is only as strong as its weakest link." You must keep reinforcing your chain links so that even your weakest link is stronger than the strongest links of your competitors. It is impossible to attain perfection, but it is not unwise to strive for it.

Yes, it is a good idea to work as a team and forge bonds to maximize output, where each member has a high point that contributes to the overall growth of the team. Business is like a jungle; there is no mercy, the strongest take it all. Make sure you surround yourself with the best players, identify constantly the bottom producers, and help them as much as possible. However, be swift with termination when they show no sign of progress.

HOW TO IDENTIFY THE DEADWOOD?

- They are always unable to achieve their goals in a consistent manner.
- They realize sporadic wins, often by pure accident.
- Their skillset is extremely unreliable
- They are use excuses to justify underperformance.
- They deliberately refuse to adjust to shifting market trends and demand.
- They are not engaged, show little initiative and are strictly reactive.
- You exhausted all your resources to help them.

As soon as you hit the last point, it is time to let them go. You can choose to move them to another department, but they cannot remain with the sales team; they are slowing the others down. They can no longer be tolerated there. It may not be their fault, they may be trying their hardest, but were not built for sales. It is not a personal decision; it is a decision for the team. If you do not make that decision, you risk losing the members of your team who are useful and efficient. They will no longer be able to tolerate the person you have refused to let go, so they will find an environment where effectiveness is demanded of everyone. Woe is you if that environment is your rival's company.

The sales management role can be extremely challenging. You are accountable to your team members, senior management, your peers, customers, vendors and business partners.

10. TRIM OFF THE DEADWOOD

If you don't take control over your calendar and prioritize tasks, you will get overwhelmed, and you will inevitably fail to lead your team to success. Your job is to drive your team members to create exceptional results by focusing on high-value strategic sales performance metrics.

ABOUT THE AUTHOR

Anthony Chaine, "A Sales Leader"

Anthony Chaine, Elite Sales Leadership Consulting, LLC, president is a sales leadership professional, skilled at assisting sales organizations on how to drive exponential revenue growth and build profitable business.

Anthony have led the creation of this community institute that focuses on helping current and future Sales Leaders. The purpose is to affect people productivity and efficiency by making informed choices and taking timely action.

Anthony spent more than 15 years in the sales management divisions of three major F500 companies. As an RVP Sales, he has guided thousands of frontline B2B salespeople and sales leaders towards optimum performance levels. He is recognized as an expert in sales management, channel management, revenue creation, performance management, training and sales forecasting.

You can catch up with Anthony here:

Contact Anthony

www.asalesleader.com

anthony@asalesleader.com

www.ingramcontent.com/pod-product-compliance
Lightning Source LLC
Chambersburg PA
CBHW031531210526
45464CB00012B/2832